FOOL

Greta Stoddart was born in 1966 in Oxfordshire. She grew up in Belgium and Oxford before going on to study drama at Manchester University, then at the École Jacques Lecoq in Paris. She co-founded the theatre company Brouhaha in London, touring the UK and Europe. She has lived in Devon since 2007.

Her first collection, *At Home in the Dark* (Anvil Press, 2001), was shortlisted for the Forward Prize for Best First Collection 2001 and won the Geoffrey Faber Memorial Prize. Her second, *Salvation Jane* (Anvil, 2008), was shortlisted for the 2008 Costa Poetry Award. In 2007 she was nominated by *Mslexia* as one of the best ten contemporary women poets in the UK. Her poem 'Deep Sea Diver' was shortlisted for the 2012 Forward Prize for Best Single Poem. Her third collection, *Alive Alive O* (Bloodaxe Books, 2015), was shortlisted for the Roehampton Poetry Prize. Her half-hour radio drama *Who's There?*, first broadcast on Radio 4's *The Echo Chamber* in 2017, was shortlisted for the Ted Hughes Award. Her fourth collection, *Fool*, was published by Bloodaxe in 2022.

GRETA STODDART

FOOL

BLOODAXE BOOKS

ISBN: 978 1 78037 627 1

First published 2022 by
Bloodaxe Books Ltd,
Eastburn,
South Park,
Hexham,
Northumberland NE46 1BS

www.bloodaxebooks.com
For further information about Bloodaxe titles
please visit our website and join our mailing list
or write to the above address for a catalogue.

Supported using public funding by
**ARTS COUNCIL
ENGLAND**

Cover design: Neil Astley & Pamela Robertson-Pearce.

Printed in Great Britain by Bell & Bain Limited, Glasgow, Scotland, on
acid-free paper sourced from mills with FSC chain of custody certification.

It is the way humans know –
through the earth, through the things of the earth

JANE HIRSHFIELD, 'Even the Vanishing Housed'

But the fool on the hill
Sees the sun going down
And the eyes in his head
See the world spinning round

PAUL McCARTNEY, 'The Fool on the Hill'

ACKNOWLEDGEMENTS

Some of these poems were first published in *Bad Lilies, Ink Sweat and Tears, The Long Poem Magazine, The Manchester Review, The North, Poetry Ireland Review, The Poetry Review* and *Poetry Wales*.

'Birds Britannica: Exhibition Catalogue' was inspired by the book *Birds Britannica* by Mark Cocker and Richard Mabey (2005) and the language found in various art exhibition catalogues. It was published in the 2021 Gingko Prize catalogue.

'Lie in a field on your back' was featured in a poem film shortlisted for the 2021 Poetry Screen Award and screened at the 2022 REEL poetry festival, Houston, Texas.

My heartfelt thanks go to Gill Barr, Elaine Beckett and Helen Evans for their invaluable critique of these poems. Also to Louise Walsh, Tinker Mather and Carol Rumens for their very helpful responses, and to Barbara Farquharson for her insights and conversations. As ever thanks to Stewart for his support which never fails and to Jesse and Frank who inspire me in so many ways.

This book is dedicated to the memory of my friend John Torrance who died while I was writing the book and who was a precious reader and fellow poet.

CONTENTS

The Act

Trouver son clown, c'est en quelque sorte se trouver soi-même

JACQUES LECOQ

I know it's been years
but I want to speak out now
for that girl who used to sit on the bench
in a shapeless frock
with an orange and brown diamond pattern
no one would seriously wear –
her hair greased and parted down the middle
her face a powdered white.
She had this look
of one who had no idea
how they might appear to others
and so without shame.
If she had a smell I know exactly what it would be –
vinegar, the last dirty bone of soap.
This is how it was:
the girl had not a single word floating inside her
or even a thought that might want to try itself out in words.
For the girl on the bench
there was some resistance to anything happening.
I mean anything at all.
She just sat there in a kind of cosmic indifference.
But soon it became clear
it was impossible to carry on like this –
it was too much for any one person to bear.
So someone laughed
then someone else did
then someone else and someone else
till the sound became enormous
and then nothing
but a big bleary drowning out
of what could not be known.

If ever you don't partake in the laughter
and so as a matter of course the tears
you'll find yourself very much alone.

So there I was
sitting on a bench
with all the humans before me
happening in the hilarious.

And if I thought anything it was this:
that I could never go to a party again
or hold someone's face in my hands
and slowly bring it in
that I might never be able to lie again
and it wouldn't be so bad to die then
being as I was so without fear
so without anything
being as I'd found who I was
in the act of being
that girl on the bench
fool that she was
for all that she didn't know.

Where to look

So let's begin
with a sweeping gesture
that it may take in
the goal-post and gate, the bird-table.

Let's call it a kind of seeking
as it goes back and forth
but really who knows
what I'm doing

except I do
keep coming back to that shrub

sitting there among the others
but somehow apart
with its small pointy leaves
and inner dark

and – were I to get closer –
its many buds each one
tightly closed but showing
the tiniest eye-slit of white.

Not that I would
– get closer that is –
I'm fine where I am
doing what I'm doing:
football, spade, tub

but it's no good –
I keep coming back to that shrub.

It's like a face in the audience
my eyes keep returning to
even though it looks half-asleep

deep in its own life
and so faraway
from what I'm trying to say...

Oh single especial shrub
you make me think
you might have the answers
you make me think
that if I continue with these sweeping gestures
you'll suddenly break out
into hundreds of little white flowers
and it'll be so beautiful
I won't know where to look.

A glass of water

So many ways of looking
at a glass of water –

why is one clearly not enough?

Because there are many ways to look
and it's a different kind of sustenance

we're after when we look at a glass of water

and maybe there's no such thing as failure

when we look
because our eyes cannot fail us –

or rather no one can say for sure
what it is they're seeing

and yet it's there before our eyes:

if we know anything we know
here is a glass in which water lies.

Why look at a thing again and again?
What are we trying to get right?

And though I know it's nothing

like the man who tried countless times
to make a light bulb

I'd like to hold one of those
failures in my hand –

see what might be done with it;
it might not have anything to do with light.

What is a question

if not the beginning of something

and what is a child
if not a beginning

alive and hurtling along towards
another question.

Here comes one now
out of the dark and full of sleep

stepping into the light
but no sooner is it out

and you begin to form
the first words of your response

– have the words even left your mouth –
than the eyes glaze over.

Of course
it was enough to ask the question.

Will you be so good
as to let it stand there

in the wide open
not knowing

will you let it grow
without your need

to tether and train
will you remain just so

and allow it to be
　　　about to become

like a flower begins
　　　to open even though

sunlight is not the answer
　　　only the reason.

Perfect Field

But then I think having all the answers
would be a bit like being dead.

What would you need to live for?

You'd be somewhere no one else was.
You'd be beyond questioning.

People would come for you and you wouldn't be there.

But being beyond questioning
is not the same as having all the answers.

It just means that you have removed yourself
(or have been removed)
from the possibility of interrogation.

Like god. Or an absolute ruler.

Or if you think about it a cat.

But to go back to being dead for a moment.

When someone dies don't you feel they
simply by that something of a miraculous vanishing act
know more than you do?

But not just anything or everything.

It's as if they have arrived
in a place of deep invulnerability
knowing only what they need to know.

There's a walk we do where we pass through
what I like to call the Perfect Field.

It's up on a high ridge
and stretches out in all directions
and the grass is bright green
and neither too short nor too long.

The children laugh at my Perfect Field
and cry 'It's not perfect, it's not a perfect field!'
and run through it chasing the dog
laughing and laughing.

I stand in the field and think
this is like being in a place beyond suffering
being so high and with such far-reaching views

but even here you can imagine
a scaffold, a badly-shot deer ...

When I am nowhere near the field
I see people kneeling in the bright grass
that stretches out in all directions.

There's a light on their faces they do not feel
and the wind that ripples through the grass
doesn't lift their hair or clothes in any way.

I don't recognise a single face.
No one knows anyone.

I don't want to see those people
kneel like that in the grass
and not feel the sun on their faces.

I don't want them to show me
how in removing themselves to the Perfect Field
they've come to know what they know
and cannot hear the laughing.

Second nature

What is a saint but a stillness. It cannot move on. But to be in humantime is to be endlessly moving. Beatification evokes a certain fixity. A date for example or a church. I would like to fix some things. Like facts. I have always been very bad at remembering facts. When I would like to be someone who has some purchase on the fundamentals. Someone for whom calling up a figure is second nature. Or not even that. Just to nail a few things down. Which is why I went and ordered this board that came with a little plastic sachet full of different-coloured pins which was in itself full of a certain kind of promise. So I have been literally pinning things down by which I mean bits of paper on which I have written not just facts but quotes and suchlike. I am very drawn to these things. They are like little windows that open into my day so I can stand there a moment and look out and have the cool wind of clarity blow through me. The board on which the scraps of paper are pinned is made of cork which makes me think of a wood I wandered through in Corsica many years ago touching as I went the rough soft bark not having realised before where cork came from. That it was even a natural thing. Which means of course that it will crumble and fall apart one day but probably long after I have stopped looking at it. Long after I have stopped looking at anything at all. But it will have served its purpose for the time being. The time being one in which I feel this need to pin things down on a cork board. Once I came across a modern-day saint in a church in Seville. I have to say I found it hard to feel reverence in front of a faded Kodak photograph. A saint is not supposed to have worn a cagoule or wandered down the aisle of a supermarket. But clearly I am out of touch. I myself stuck in a past of gloomy churches and flat impassive faces. What are saints anyway but our own better selves following some fierce instinct right to the brink of self. But mildly of course and with humility. They were once flesh and bone like us. Some bled like us and had to deal with that. Peer down at the blood on the cloth and deal with that. *You will find something more in woods than in books. Trees and stones will teach you that which you can never learn from masters* says Saint Bernard on one scrap of paper I've looked at so many times I no longer know what it means. It's like that gold-wrapped Easter egg we placed on the shelf and kept putting off eating until such a time as we felt we deserved it so that it just kept sitting there and with each day that passed we desired it less and less and no longer understood what it meant to want it in the way we once had. I love the way there are many different ways of arriving at a thing. I love the fact that miracles have to be approved by a board. Once dead you have to pass another kind of test: did you or did you not cure that 3-year-old of its vegetative state? Dear María de la Purísma Salvat Romero you were undoubtedly a good woman. One who peered down at the cloth and saw blood. You have your date. You may even get a church. Or they might make of you a figurine which they will place on a shelf for children to stop and look at and some will touch you and even though they will have been told to be good and be sure to pray to you they will one day find themselves in a wood through which they'll wander and find they are touching a tree here and a stone there for it will have become second nature to them to enquire of a stillness – touch briefly upon its meaning – before moving on

Three tulips in a milk bottle

Of course I'd like there to be meaning
– who wouldn't? – look how I just said that
with barely a pause to imagine a person
for whom meaning would be a mere sideshow

but now that I have
I can't help but see her –

there she is
fixing three tulips in a milk bottle,
her eyes shifting this way and that,
standing back for a moment
before stepping in to make small changes.

No, it's not that I'd *like* there to be no meaning,
it's simply that I don't feel it
or if I could just stand back for a moment:

no thing has any inherent meaning
and perhaps we'd do as well to accept that

– or more, actually lie down
contentedly in the mud with that,
feel how warm and happy it is
in the ramshackle enclosure
under the good grey sun
with its big rotten fruit
chucked in at irregular intervals –

or if that's unbearable
(and believe me I do understand)
then by all means go and write

a little something to explain
that all meaning is made –

and you can say what you like here
but you might mention the arranging of the tulips;

say how beautiful that person
must have found them
growing there in the garden,
how she couldn't resist the urge
to pick them and bring them in,

make a thing of them but
no matter what she did they wouldn't stand,
they simply wouldn't stand
for what she had in mind.

Clay

And so it was
more and more
(is that too strong?)
of going back
to walk
that old dirt path
that damp stone smell
that length of thin
slumped
of a sun-sharp
deep in the shade
of the old steel factory
all but one
chunking out the last rivets
in that
in which I knew
that it might hurt
and had my heart
by all that was and was
how would I bear
spring smell
early evening smell
before its time
but then it came
nobody made me
there with time
to my life
by any particular person
so there I was
towards that place (my
when I fell in step
carrying a red bucket
in the other
all new
and as I slowed

with every passing year
the fear
yes the fear
knowing it might hurt
back along
beside the canal
in early spring
brown water
in the dark
day
of the high brick wall
with its windows broken
still lit
of the century
soft historical dusk
even then I knew
the day I went back
rearranged
no longer there
that sudden blossoming
the clay and damp
that place old
its line of dead water
I knew it would
just one day
and a certain indifference
as a thing lived
including myself
walking the path
heart starting to go a little)
behind a man
in one hand
a blue mop
and wrapped in plastic
and stared at the back

of his crumpled suit
about the man
he realised
that no one else
and the time had come
walking towards
at the newly-converted
where a floor
and I knew
that no matter what
how many times
and forth
it would never
not like it was
before
or before
still warm
or before before
upon whose surface
afraid

I started to think
and the moment
that he was the one
was going to do it for him
so here he was
what had to be done
factory flats
lay waiting
and perhaps he did too
he did no matter
he went back
with the mop
be the same again
when it was first laid down
all the walking
when it was just tiles piled up on pallets
from the cutting
when it was part of the damp earth
a person would walk
they might get hurt

Slow Cinema

You're late
but it doesn't matter with this one
says the man just go on in
and the place is empty
so the film's showing to no one
and as it happens it happens
to be showing
an empty auditorium
much like the one you've just sat down in
with a stand of red raked seats
and a side door in the left wall
which after a while opens
and a woman walks in
with a brace – or boot –
on one foot
which makes a loud clumping sound
as she walks slowly across the floor
in front of the seats.
You feel the weight of it
as she climbs the central steps
lifting it behind her
before she turns down a row
and bends to pick something up
then straightens and walks slowly
back along the row
back down the steps
placing the braced foot carefully down before her
as if it were the most important part
of her body
(which being damaged
you could say it was)
and back she goes
along the front of the seats
and out the side door
leaving you sitting there

in the empty auditorium
watching the red seats
and listening to the silence
which now she has left it has changed.
If anything it is more whole.
What it had been waiting for
has happened so now
it can fold in on itself
and open out –
fold in on itself
and open out ...
oh what is this mystery that is
another person who is
essentially you
who haven't dared go back
to look for the lost thing
for fear of the sound
your heart would make
fear that if you found it
it would mean nothing
and everything
would be the same.

Adult Education

She is old enough to be my mother.
I'm afraid of what she'll say next.
She has what she herself would never say
(because it is a cliché) –
a 'formidable intellect'.
There are things in her life
that have made her sad and formless.
Everything falls.
I find myself clucking and cooing over her.
Once I touched her arm.
I am a fool.
I'm afraid of her saying to me
'That is simply not true'
and me knowing it.
My mind jumps up and down in its bag
and wants to get out
when she walks in the room.
When she says my name
(which is not at all often)
I feel – briefly – of some worth.
She once said to me
'I should like to hear you on Auden'
and I lay awake composing
a cold and brilliant talk
called *About Suffering*
which I had myself telling her
over tea in the canteen.
There are things in her life –
but there's never time.
I watch her shuffle out
with her plastic bags full
of fourteenth-century Italian poetry
which is the class she goes to after mine.

Fool

Look at your desk,
can't you see it's had enough
of your elbows, your head, your heart –

break it up and feed the fire
for the Fool is nothing

if not drawn to the bright spark
in all dying things

Then let the Fool in foolish dress
make awkward gestures of tenderness

Let us in this way
be entertained in all manner
of small mercies

Let us be grateful for them
and for the Fool who is nothing
if not good

for nothing is what we're good for
nothing might be what is called for

How I come to clean the windows

So this is how it is:
these endless moments that end so quickly –
how to tend to them all.

See how that wasn't a question:
I put it to myself as a quest with a very small q.

This is what happens at a certain point:
an easing of ambition (phew) and now just this

queasy nonchalance that comes from all the being
there each morning
to greet the rolling delivery of days.

A spider scuttles across the back of my hand –
whyever do I let it.

Take it to mean that I mean well
when really it is to me as I am to it,
as rain is to the glass.

Poor windows who are so functional and calm,
who keep it all in who keep it all out,
who suffer the endless moments of rain.

Go little spider go!
Make a dash for the place you have in your tiny blue mind

for I have these windows to see to.
They could be so large and bright.

Smile

I know there are worse things
than a smile

that doesn't reach the eyes
but it's hard

to think of a sadder way
of saying it's hopeless

or in this particular instance
we are without hope.

But it's also a way of saying
I suffer you

or that thing you just said
or made me do.

And wouldn't you say it's an act
of passive aggression

in that it wants to hurt the one
who's just done the hurt by saying

I'm not going to show you
how I really feel.

And it is of course a way of saying
I am not happy

which is not an easy thing to say
but if you put a spin on it

in the form of a smile
that doesn't quite do it

it might possibly mean
that you'd like to be.

But when we're alone
we must simply endure –

stand at the window
and lose ourselves

in the birds feeding
and fighting each other off the feeder.

Birds Britannica: Exhibition Catalogue

The vivid display
>of high-keyed colour suggests an acidic immediacy
that contrasts playfully with the Lesser-Spotted
Woodpecker's deep connection to more elemental
scapes such as ancient glades and old cider orchards,
whose subtle and diverse varieties of dead wood
recreated here offer the ideal context.

Muted tones and lost histories
>are interwoven in the vision of the Grey Partridge,
who likes to ask how a future ruralism might present
itself, attracted as she is to pastoral tropes such as
the swing of a rusty gate or open ploughed ground,
which she seeks to express by colours dull and delicate,
sudden deft twists.

What begins as a dialogue
>between folk tale and woodcut becomes the
haunting starting point for the Barn Owl but one
from which he may deviate for in some cultures
the owl is considered a fool, an idea perceived
here as something to both honour and subvert.

Typically grounded
>in the process of collating variations of local visual
phenomena – the more surprising the combination
the better – the Magpie gathers objects that, while
accruing unstable symbolisms, act as physical
footnotes to an entire era.

A shy and quiet spirit
           the Wood Warbler aims to frustrate the process
           of recognition by treading a path almost lost among
           wet leaves and dead bracken, between the borders of
           figuration and abstraction.

We see in his body
           of work materials as diverse as charcoal, plastic and
           greaseproof paper, which the Herring Gull uses to
           employ a sense of provisionality as he explores how the
           built environment is both source and trap alongside
           which the liminal offers a deep ambiguous charge that
           could be described as a sort of despairing triumphalism.

Tracing her beginnings
           in classical still life the Mute Swan emerges from
           myths of decadence and mortality set against a
           background overpainted with lakes and rivers, where
           she presents a facade at once closed but pervious to
           a kind of fixed interiority.

What is being proposed
           by the Song Thrush is a way of imagining how
           the concrete might be released into a more fluid
           understanding of time and space.

Appearing here as a form
           of semi-erased expression, the Skylark represents
           himself as lone symbol that manages to exalt the idea
           of how a national identity might exist more fully in
           art than in a vanishing reality.

Insisting that violence too

> must be accommodated the Cuckoo operates between acts
> of damage and reparation and while keen to explore
> notions of parasitic exploitation she nonetheless celebrates
> opportunity and daring together with a certain brash self-
> preservation, where any nagging doubts about the means of
> creating are always overcome by the promise of something
> new.

As part of her continuing interest

> in participatory art the Nightingale asks that we take
> ourselves to the edge of a wood and listen and in the
> unlikely event that we will hear anything may we
> nonetheless make ourselves open to the possibility that
> something might be heard thereby allowing ourselves to
> become the artwork in the way we stand there in the dark
> listening for what is no longer there.

Cold and lonely wastes

It's easy to forget how
the sun is constantly
burning somewhere in
black space and that like
us it has a life which means
that one day it will die

but when it does it will
expand and its dying light
will radiate and spread out
to touch even the furthest
planets that lie in the cold
and lonely wastes

Oh mother I am afraid
we don't like it when
you say you're done that
you've had a long life but
now you're tired can't you
see we're hardwired to
want to keep you alive

Please hear us when we
say we want to stay as long
as we can in your
radiance exhausted
though we know it is

We want time to imagine
how it will be and what
we'll find when we cup
our hands in the new
silvery pools not knowing
if it's good to drink or if
it will sustain us

Concorde

When actually what I really want
to talk about is after the accident
when for a whole year
I was carried by my mother
to various houses
to lie on a sofa for the day.

I remember one in particular
which had a small galley kitchen
with a woman inside it
clattering around quite cheerful I think
always doing something.

I suppose she was looking after me.
I suppose that is what she was doing
making me a sandwich or something.

But what I remember most
is watching Concorde take off
again and again.

It was the first commercial flight
so it was taking off with people inside it.
People who had paid to be inside it
eat steak and drink champagne.

I didn't know any of that then.
All I knew was that it had taken off
which was something they wanted to show us
again and again

in order perhaps that we might begin
to imagine those inside it
what they were doing
and what that might be like

and why wasn't it us inside it
and what had we done with our lives
that had led us to the point
where we knew in our hearts
we'd only ever be the ones to watch
and imagine.

So let's imagine

I'm the woman in the kitchen
clattering around
cutting the bread
asking myself what led me
to take in this child
lying there without a word

while inside her body
her poor broken bones
are slowly coming back together
but ever so slightly differently

and I know because I do
because I'm the woman in the kitchen now
what's going on for that child

by which I mean anyone
who can't help but be broken

as they lie transfixed
by the world out there
the way it keeps happening
to them and not to them

how there'll always be this trying
to mend what's within
with all that is without.

The little living room

When I was nine
a family came to live inside me.
I'd lie in my bed at night and tune in
to what would always be the end of the day there
as if they too had been out and about in the world
and were now safely back and ready to bed down.
The children would run squealing
down the long corridors of my legs
being chased by their father
while mother would be in the kitchen
that was my belly that was
the warm and churning centre of the home
and when father had tucked them all in
and was sitting at the end of a bed
looking down at the floor
mother would come
and lay a hand on his shoulder
and together they'd walk back up the corridor
through the kitchen
that sat there in its air of detergent and cooked meat
turning lights off as they went
and when they came to the wooden spiral staircase
that began at the base of my ribs
they'd pause so that father could indicate with his hand
that she was to go and he follow
which she would but not without
a glance up to the rafters
to check that all was good and solid up there
that everything would hold
at least for another night
and so they'd climb up
into the little living room of my heart
where they'd sit in chairs and rock gently back and forth
and murmur about the day that had been
and who'd said what

and wasn't that one funny and that one loud
and wasn't that one quiet
and why was that they wondered
were you born like that
no matter how good the home how happy
and they'd sit there
in the fug and warmth of my heart
not knowing and the fire would be dying down
and all the lively shadows returning to the corners
and I'd have to make an effort to stay awake here
because I wanted to keep listening
I really wanted to know
I may even have sat up
I may even have got out of bed
but the parents would be up and walking along
the short passage of my neck where
because it was always colder
at this end of the house
a heavy brown curtain hung
which the father would pull sharply across
making that tearing thin-metal-hooped sound
and into their bed they'd climb
somewhere inside
the soft interior of my brain
where they'd lie on their backs
and stare at the ceiling
and the whole house would be quiet
inside me who was quiet
kneeling in front of the fire
feeding it furniture
I remember breaking at some point
into hundreds of little pieces.

School Field

The thin green bar from the aquarium
where two turtles sat staring
lovelessly into space
not eating their lettuce
was the only light beyond the stars
that night as it cast a pool
over the school field
where two children lay on their backs
gazing up at the sky.
'Immortality,' he whispered and she agreed
on the lovely sound of the word.
It was a time of new vocabularies
which they handed to each other carefully:
cosmic, manic depression, irony.
Then they lay in silence.
Then he placed himself on top of her.
'You get the stars,' he said
as if she were supposed to be grateful
which in a way she was.
The boy went on to physics, opera, God.
She became a clown.
How absurd our futures once we've lived them!
For now though let's leave this pair
in the middle of the playing field
in whatever they are making
out of first love. Soon it will break
and no longer contain just the two
of them and what they don't
know will never be known
this closely again.

Remote

A man is prodding something on a grill
using a long pair of tongs.
A boy is holding a blue book
whose cover has the words
Heroes of Olympus in yellow.
There's a woman too and she is holding a glass.
'I like the idea of a cool red,'
she says to no one in particular.
Perhaps she doesn't even say it.
A low brick wall runs around the property.
They have paid a substantial amount
to feel a certain kind of exclusivity and it's true
the wall goes some way to doing that.
You know where you are
and also – just there over the wall – where you are not.
It's also been incredibly hot.
This too is something they have paid for
and the pool with its constant low functioning hum.
Everything is quiet now it's evening –
even the boy who is deep in the making
it more complicated and clarification that is literature.
But I don't want to make too much of that here.
I want to watch the woman sip her drink
and not think. I want to be here
where there's a pair of large electric gates
that open very slowly and very slowly close
so that each of their comings and goings
has become something of a ritual
as if the move from here to there
were full of significance
and laborious to achieve.
Sometimes the boy likes to play with the remote
– pause the gates at a particular point
so that they're neither open nor closed
which his parents don't like.

His father gets angry: 'What are you doing?'
and there's a moment of bright tension
as the boy looks up at the man
because it's perfectly clear to him what he's doing
with the gates suspended there
in time and the space
between them probably just enough for him
– and he'd love this, their little fleet-footed one –
to slip through and run down the lane holding
the remote up high, turning to laugh at them
stranded there behind the gates.

Constellation

So the boy was put right
in the middle of a circle
he normally stood outside

and strangers were moved
here and there at various
angles and distances to him

and when it was done and they all
stood in the hall newly arranged
in the light and dust

he felt like one
who'd just been shown
but with a certain care

that it was the planets who moved
around the sun
that he was in fact the sun

and how wrong that felt to him
being there and all the faces
looking in and how could he be

the centre being so small
how to hold it all or know what
to do who to hide behind

when a man stepped slowly
forward to be his mother
and the boy felt his love for her

in all its complicatedness
and knew that it wasn't a question
of right or wrong

that it wasn't a question of anything
being only what
had been there all along

but obscured by the old alignment
and that it wasn't looking for answers
or even a response

needing only to show itself
so the boy would know the truth
in what was not true:

him in the centre facing
his mother who was not
his mother but a man with love

he hadn't known was his to give
until he found himself
standing in the boy's light.

Consider the mornings

Consider the mornings we've woken into
     and you turn to me
     or I to you
     and why it is
     I still prefer to wake alone
     it's something about the light
     how it brings
     a certain clarity of tone
     after the weight and dread of the night

Consider the night
     the one time we see ourselves
     in space
     so wonder what we are
     how for example
     the fundamental laws of physics
     can't explain the on/off beauty of your face
     but can how the electricity
     I find in stroking you
     is there too in a star

Consider electricity
     and at the same time
     the eternal mystery
     how science is only possible
     because of it
     how nature likes to complicate itself
     inside the vast simplicity of its plan:
     think eye of an insect, love of a man
     how compound and complex

Consider the last time
       we'll ever have sex
       you and I
       how we live among things destined to die:
       that man's love, that insect eye

Consider your being
       destined to die
       how of course I'll cry
       but at the same time think
       how different it feels
       when taken outside
       how commonplace and wide
       it'll be something about the light
       compared to how the mind is
       so compound and complex

Consider the eternal mystery
       and how it might be
       absolutely devoid of love and yet
       how potential is that *yet*

Consider a temperate self-possessed approach to disaster
       how absurd and yet
       potential is that
       clarity of tone

Consider that tone
       the one to take
       the morning when
       I or you
       will wake alone
       and it'll no longer be
       a matter of preference
       nor will it be a disaster
       but commonplace and wide
       as you or I
       will step outside
       where something about the light
       after the weight of the night
       will make us wonder
       what we are
       and at the same time
       how electricity in a star
       is only possible
       because of the eternal yet
       vast simplicity of the plan:
       think eye of an insect, love of a man

Once upon a time

there was a word
that was sick of its meaning
the way it was said and said
like a wet cloth carelessly slapping a table.
What a tearjerker of a word it was.
It barely knew what it meant anymore
like it had collapsed from over-usage.
Poor old thing
who more than any other word
felt it had to be what it was
really only supposed to be about.
Why carry on
when they said it who didn't mean it
when they meant it who didn't say it.
It all made the word feel pretty existential about itself.
Maybe if it could stop meaning
the feeling would be set free!
But in the end it knew
that whatever it was
was made in the moment
by those who found themselves there
who found the word wanting
only to prove itself
in the silent moving air.

Untimely

(for Polly)

But doesn't everything that happens
happen absolutely in time?

Not that I want to suggest a kind of fatalism
as if time were a baseline along which various events
were marked as being expected
at more or less the same intervals.

Time has no time for such things.
Time is all over the place
much to our great sorrow.

It holds us, it lets us go

the way a cloud is most perfectly
an old woman's face
then slowly it is not.

How slow and suddenly it is gone,
is just cloud moving on.

So there was this girl.
She was dark and in her darkness lay
a knowing beyond her years.

There's a picture of her standing
on some stone steps by a canal.

She has become very specific in the picture
in a long red velvet dress
and golden crown made of card.

She is staring into the brown water.

Time is happening in all sorts of ways
as I stare at the picture at her
staring into the brown water.

And now that look has come to mean something

though nothing was meant in that moment;
there were some steps, a red dress,
maybe a promise of ice cream.

But time has come to rest here.
It insists on what we cannot understand
so we look and look.

Time is nothing if not timely
and anything that happens in time
also happens outside it:

so a girl dies on 26th June 2007 in a children's ward in Turin

but also somewhere
that has no name or mark or meaning

and she was going to die the moment she was born
like us all

and she dies each time one of us remembers
she is dead.

A deer flowing over the hedge
happens in that moment
and all moments to come
where a deer flows over a hedge

and every time you walk past the hedge
and there isn't a deer in sight.

A life of seven years is a complete life.

(This is something we had to learn, we didn't know it then.)

It even had its longeurs and boredoms.
She made things and threw them away.
There was a daily give and take of love.
She was one of the lucky ones.

And no school – just hours and hours of drawing
nurses with haloes,
a child holding an enormous bunch of flowers
with great affection.

Once she gave me a little golden laughing Buddha.
I have him here on my desk.
He appears to have difficulty standing up.
He likes to keel over laughing
especially when things don't work out
the way I want them to
and I'm swearing and hitting out at stuff.

He just lies there on his back
with his palm on his fat little golden belly
looking up at the ceiling and laughing.

And there's a clock on the wall.

And there's a deer flowing over the hedge
even though I am nowhere near
a deer flowing over a hedge

just as I am nowhere near

the girl on the steps
in her red dress and cardboard crown
staring into the brown water.

And this was my abiding thought towards the end
when I'd pick up the phone to her mother:

you'll soon hold your dead child in your arms:
how can you live in a present that contains such a future?

And after when I'd sink down on the stairs and lose
myself in useless pity and fret I'd see her
put the phone down and walk across
to the table where her daughter would be drawing
one of her figures administering love

(as an artist this was her recurring theme)

sit there with her to start in
on the scatter of pencils that needed sharpening
and say, 'You've got that hand there, the one
holding the sick bird, you've got it just right.'

Walking into church

is like walking
into someone's mind.

I don't know how to think or be,
how to look in the slant light.

I'm being watched. Am I being watched.
What is being thought of me.

I want to lay myself down at the feet
of someone who might do something.

What am I saying.
Who is listening.

Only the silence
that's been made over the years by those

who've come to weigh their grief in the air,
left the light thick with it.

Say it: you are not alone.
I am not alone, I say.

Won't you take me in, old thing
or forgive me at least for I know not

what I'm doing planting a candle
in this melting glimmering tray.

Spell

Only this morning you swore you saw
something swift and white fly through the night
and land on the gate in the dark.

And now you're saying you think you saw
a bluebell begin to realise what it was among the many
which is a singular but not a special part.

Why am I not surprised.
We always think beyond what we can see.
Like now, I think I know what you're thinking:

that it feels like a curse or some sort of spell
that we can't seem to tell how things are
from how we make them out to be?

What's real – touch me and you'll know
I'm just another thing pushing up
out of the earth to claim its one mortal place

wanting to hear again what you believe
came flying through the night
with its wide open face.

The long grass

Such a fragile thing of such fragile quickness disappearing into the long grass. What is it what is it. Everyone's pointing and shouting. Why is everyone so angry? Why this kicking and kicking it into the long grass? Some are shouting and some running and some just drive smoothly by. Smile and wave – do I know you? Quiet mornings if you know where to look, or even if you don't, you'll see something sidestep across the rug on soundless legs. What is it what is it. Only what's happening now. But what is that? It is what it is, say those who drive smoothly by. But don't they feel it, don't you feel it? I mean what a strange time this is. I don't mean this particular moment here between you and me. I mean all the others – like the ones that move without a sound across the rug casting their long shadows – the ones I don't do anything with when I could be running and shouting and kicking them into the long grass. What am I doing here staring at the moments as they move and gather, gather and move, until there comes a point – enough is enough – I roll them up inside the rug and take them out and burn them. To hell with all those moments when all I do is sit and watch. Why is everyone so angry? What is it what is it. It is what it is, say those who drive smoothly by on their way to somewhere. We've all been there, haven't we, sealed and seated and going nowhere. Moving gently as move we must. Come on, they say, tell us what it's like, they say, tell us how it is – as if they didn't know. Don't they know? Don't they see the running and the shouting, don't they see those moments on the rug? Because I can't, I can't tell it. I don't know what it is. Or is it this: like being in a state of forever losing something. Not just the minutes in the morning but the possibility of ever knowing a true thing. There it goes into the long grass. There goes me running after it and there goes someone slowly driving by. Stop – do I know you? What's that burning? What is it what is it. It is what it is, they say and smile and wave as that thing of fragile, of such fragile quickness, disappears into the long grass.

Performance

I'm sitting at an open window
in a new light
wondering why it is
that when I write
I sometimes seem to know
more than I actually do –
some fool out there
keeps falling down and getting up
and trying hard
to make me laugh
but I want to stay inside
and ask myself
if this is true.
Because I don't feel I know
very much at all
but my poems – look at them
waving their inky little hands in the air!
Watch me take a word,
a single word
like *defenestration*
and consider it
in a cold structural way
which is to say
without thinking of a body
throwing itself out of a window
for what's lodged deep inside it
to make its great escape.
There I go again.
Please understand
that is not what I want
for the body – I want it to land,
brush itself down and keep
on with the show.

Flowers for my ego and a dark stage

with a single beam of light
not on me I hasten to add
but a dream I have
where I'm curled right down
in a corner of the universe
and what's crowding me out
what's bearing down on me
while I'm being the only living thing
down there in space
is a vast dark mind
I'm given to understand
over time is mine
and that foetal floating lost thing
no one will ever find
is me who I was
before I came
to play the part
I was born to play
so tell me
who is that
smiling and bowing
in the vast dark hall
wondering where everyone's gone
and where the fuck are my flowers?

The Rose Garden

How courteous he was and gentle
when he welcomed me into the garden

and as he took the coat delicately from my shoulders
I had the sense of being admitted
into a sect of some complexity which wasn't
as it happened an unpleasant feeling;

the ease of suddenly belonging to something
while having my identity painlessly erased

didn't seem to matter in the slightest –
what did I ever know about that anyway.

A bird was singing high in a tree.
He remarked on its remarkable cadences.
He seemed to have a genuine respect for the creature
that included how inconsequential you could argue it was.

He pointed out the different roses in Latin.
I thought who'd have thought
the man has an eye for beauty but then
I wondered who didn't.

'The problem is,' he was saying, his nose in a rose, 'everything has a price'.

'Omnia pretia habent,' he said, in case I hadn't understood the first time.

And though he wasn't exactly shy
he seemed to want to play down all that he was
and shine a little glory light on me.

Strange how in that garden
I began to feel calm and cleansed

as if I were becoming innocent again;
is such a thing possible, I wonder.

We sat on a bench and listened to the bird.

I stared into the shiny dark leaves in front of me.
They were easier to look at than the roses.

What was I doing there.

I'd been sent to help him
with the beginnings of a new language.

There might be something in it for me,
is what I'd thought.

So there I was
sitting next to the man I knew perfectly well
had done a number of questionable things.

'Questionable,' they'd said, 'depends on who's asking the question.'

How could he,
is what I'd thought.

But now I was here inside the garden
I knew exactly how he could
seeing as how remote and enclosed it was
and how the little bird poured itself into the air …

He was very quiet sitting there beside me.
He whom I'd only ever seen talking,

who no matter what he appeared to be talking about
was always talking about power;
as if it were something he wanted others to have,
as if he wanted them to go and get it,
take it upon themselves to go all out and get it

but all they did was fall at his feet
believing he was the one to give it.

'Quid faciam?' he murmured, 'quid faciam?'

And as I sat there beside him on the bench
I became aware of something
I thought

that by staring hard into the dark leaves
I might be able to bring
into focus

a thing on his lap
a piece of pale flesh
no longer than a thumb
lying there inert and without purpose.

Did he want me to touch it.
What did he want me to do.

All I knew was that I wasn't afraid
now that I had my innocence back
and knew what it was.

I heard a flapping overhead.
I heard the leaves breathe.

Where was I supposed to find the beauty now.

And as he sat there he seemed to become abstracted
from what lay between his legs
as if he no longer knew what it was

or wanted to put some distance
between himself and it,

wanted us both to pause,
contemplate it

as it was now
in that moment between us,
peaceable and small
not asking for anything but to be seen
in its soft sleeping state.

I wish I could be 'fresh, honest and brave'

But I'm as desiccated as an old date.
I lie like a snake in the grass
and as for bravery
every night I stand
on the hard surface of the earth
knowing only
that as far as I can see
tomorrow will surely come trailing clouds
and it's all I can do
to believe it.

Yesterday I planted a tree

is a line I wrote this morning.
It also happens to be the truth.
The truth!

A train swooshes past.
A cow big and solid stares out:
what am I doing in this field?

is what I have the cow saying
because of that look she has
which has something of me at this moment in it.

Shall I carry on – look at the tree
and think of ways to conjure it
even though it's already there.

Come the afternoon all this will appear
faintly ridiculous – like the moon in daytime:
what in the world are you doing?

is what I have the moon saying
because of that look she has
which has something of me at this moment in it.

Come cow come moon
oh come the afternoon
when it will be time

to get up and comb my hair in a way
I never have before to see
if it makes any difference.

I scoop dirt from my fingernails.
Yesterday was a good day.
My hands pushed deep into the earth.

What is a tree

but
the simple fact
of itself
there each morning
when you open the curtains
is it really unchanged from the night before
you can't tell
all you know is one day
you'll look and its leaves will be gone
something will rise in your throat
you'll throw your hands up in the air
(that old gesture)
and cry
how did I not
see that coming
how did I not
see that tree
lose its last precious leaf
and will I not
take comfort now
in the simple fact
that it's nothing
nothing
to do with grief

My life came up to me and said

'I want to ask you about courage.'

It wasn't a good time.
I was kneeling at the iris bed.
I'd been waiting weeks to do this –

to not think about anything
but the irises and my need
to free them of all
the nettles and wild grasses,
my need to cut a border,

look out the window
and feel a deep satisfaction
at the sight of the dark dug-over soil,
broken now and open,
ready for the rain to enter,

for the green sheaths to push up,
unfurl their purple flags to the air.

'Do you think you have more
because of the years or less?'

And I looked at my life as I have always done
– askance, sceptical – and said:

'I'm not sure I ever had it.
I'm not sure you asked for it.
Things happened that made me
sad as the next person
but my choices were clear to me
and I was always able to make them.'

'Do you know how lucky you are?' my life said,
placing a hand on my shoulder
as I looked down and scraped my trowel with a stick.

I have no idea why the tears came.
I didn't know who to thank
or if even thanks were due –
surely not to my life who,
I could see now, was simply passing by.

Lie in a field on your back

Lie in a field on your back and
        look
before you leap into your
        mind
you don't say a single thing more
        for now
there is nothing and all is
        behind you
is a black dog
        sitting
still is the body's way of saying
        patience
is a game you play when you want to feel
        dead
or alive both are hard because of the
        nights
are worse when you have to lie there and
        count
on the fingers of one
        hand
over your heart for it is your one earthly
        belonging
has never felt like an easy thing to
        do
unto others especially the ones you don't
        know
thyself to be an unfathomable
        construct
a life then stand back and watch it
        fall
then rise like a miracle
        look
it is a miracle
        look

before you leap in to what it
        means
to an end is what this is all
        about
thinking we are never completely
        wrong
one minute right
        the next
time you'll get to see how things
        are
you sure there is only one
        way
over your head is the sky so
        lie
until you find the truth in the
        lie
in a field on your
        back
to what you think this is and
        look
while you can you
        fool
yourself you understand